福 **Fu** (foo): blessing

飞 **Fay** (fay): to fly

羊 **Yang** (yong): sheep or goat

山 **Shan** (shon): mountain

Scripture taken from the NEW AMERICAN STANDARD BIBLE®, Copyright © 1960, 1962, 1963, 1968, 1971, 1972, 1973, 1975, 1977, 1995 by The Lockman Foundation. Used by permission.

ISBN: 978-0-9970439-4-5

2 3 4 5 6 7 8 9 10 LEO 24 23 22 21 20 19 18

Printed In China

TALES FROM FuFu's FOREST

The Courage to Obey

True Stories
Told by Fictional Characters

By Eugene Bach & Amy Parker

Illustrated by Hopeful

BACK TO
归耶路撒冷
JERUSALEM

On the tip-top of a mountain, in a tiny village, a boy named Shan lived on the edge of a bamboo forest.

Every morning, Shan's parents rose with the sun and headed out to work in the fields. And every morning, Shan would stand at the door and wave until they disappeared into the hills below.

It was then that Shan would get a little lonely . . . and maybe even a little scared.

He tried to stay busy until his parents returned.

He got dressed and made his bed, washed dishes and swept the floor.

But well before the sun had climbed to the top of the sky, Shan often sat there alone, staring out at the valley below.

"I wonder . . . ," he said to himself one day, mustering his courage.

Then he jumped up, pulled on his rain boots, and ran out the door.

Shan stopped at the edge of a tall, green wall. "Is that . . . *music*?" he whispered, shaking off a chill.

The bamboo swayed overhead, and its narrow leaves danced in the wind. Shan swayed along, until suddenly, the sun seemed to point him to an opening that was just his size. Shan looked left, looked right, and stepped through the arch of bamboo.

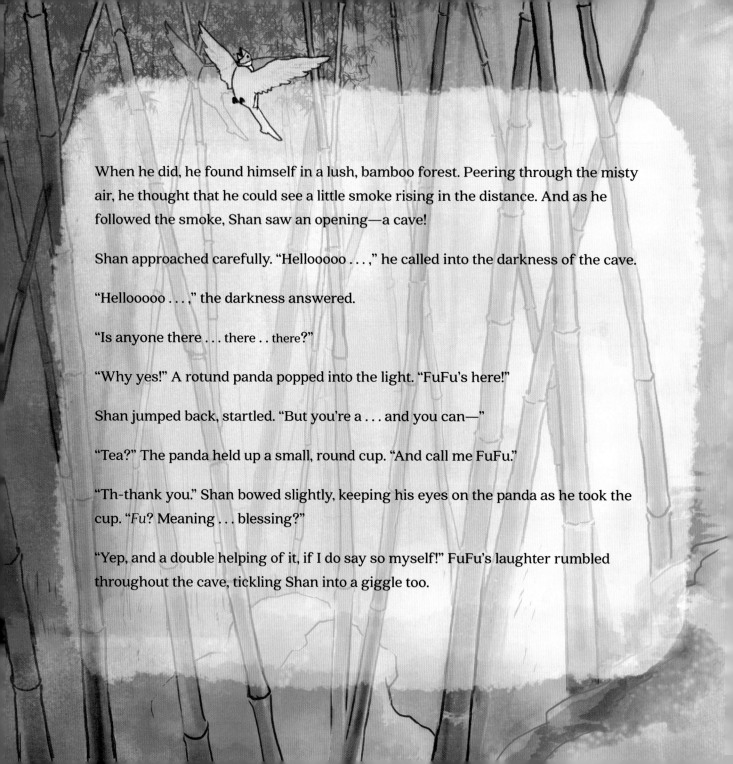

When he did, he found himself in a lush, bamboo forest. Peering through the misty air, he thought that he could see a little smoke rising in the distance. And as he followed the smoke, Shan saw an opening—a cave!

Shan approached carefully. "Hellooooo . . . ," he called into the darkness of the cave.

"Hellooooo . . . ," the darkness answered.

"Is anyone there . . . there . . there?"

"Why yes!" A rotund panda popped into the light. "FuFu's here!"

Shan jumped back, startled. "But you're a . . . and you can—"

"Tea?" The panda held up a small, round cup. "And call me FuFu."

"Th-thank you." Shan bowed slightly, keeping his eyes on the panda as he took the cup. "*Fu*? Meaning . . . blessing?"

"Yep, and a double helping of it, if I do say so myself!" FuFu's laughter rumbled throughout the cave, tickling Shan into a giggle too.

Shan and FuFu settled into cozy conversation. They talked about their parents and their homes and their friends, of which Shan had very few. Then they talked about their hopes and fears, of which Shan had quite a few.

"I try to be brave," he began, "but when I'm sitting home alone, I start thinking, what if something happens? What if my parents are hurt in the field? What if they never come home? What if—"

"Whoaaa there, little guy! That's enough to scare anybody!" FuFu stretched an arm around Shan.

"There will be no worrying on my watch!" a voice chirped from above. A little Sichuan jay settled on Shan's knee and took a bow.

"Well, hey there, Miss Fay!" FuFu reached out his paw, and the bird hopped on. "Where've you been? Who'd you see?"

"Tibet," she answered FuFu, and then turned to Shan, "where I just happened to meet an amazingly brave woman, Sister Li."

"Oh boy." FuFu stood and shuffled into the cave. "We're gonna need another pot of tea."

Fay took the table as her stage and began. "So, Sister Li—"

"Now, hold your horses, there, Fay." A takin had now joined their party. Behind the animal, Shan could see a path that led to another home—sort of a half house, half rocket?—nestled into the trees beside the cave.

"I wanna hear the news from Tibet too," the takin said, then elbowed Shan. "That's my old stompin' grounds, ya know."

"Yes, yes, Yang." Fay batted her eyelashes at the interruption. "As I was saying, Sister Li was a missionary in Liaoning." She pulled a map from her bag and tapped a spot in northeastern China. "She had just gotten married when God spoke to her very clearly."

Fay leaned in close and her voice grew softer. "God told her, 'My daughter, I want you to go to Tibet to tell others about Me.' Sister Li couldn't believe what she was hearing! She was terrified. She knew her husband wouldn't approve. And she was right."

"Sister Li kept God's message to herself for a while. But she knew: she had to tell her husband. And just as she expected, he refused to go with her. 'The people in Tibet hate us Han Chinese!' he yelled at his wife. 'If you go, then you go alone.'

"Sister Li did not want to leave her new husband or her family. She was afraid of traveling to Tibet all alone, but she knew what she must do. Through tears, she wrote a letter, telling her husband that she would be obedient to the task God had called her to do. Then she would quickly return home to him."

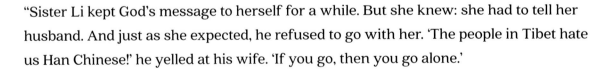

FuFu handed steaming cups of tea to his friends, but no one looked away from Fay. She walked across her map and tapped Tibet.

"Hundreds of miles later in Tibet, Sister Li looked around and asked, 'Well, God . . . what now?' Just then, she passed a pile of burlap blankets and noticed a hand reaching out from the bottom of that pile. She didn't think much of it until God told her, 'Go give that person a hug.' 'The person under the blankets? A hug?' she wondered. But again, she obeyed.

"When Sister Li lifted the blankets, a young woman hid her face. Sister Li could see that a skin disease had seriously deformed the face and arms of the young woman. Regardless, Sister Li did what God had told her to do: she gave the young woman a hug."

FuFu stood frozen with a pot of tea in hand. Shan gasped, and Yang clapped his hooves, but Fay wasn't finished yet.

"But Sister Li knew that she had to do more. She found a place for them to live, then fed the young woman, put medicine on her skin, and prayed for her day after day. One morning a few weeks later, the woman screamed from her room, and Sister Li ran to see what was wrong. 'I'm healed! I am healed!' the woman cried. Sister Li looked her over—her face and arms were completely healed. The woman's skin disease was gone!

"Immediately, the young lady wanted to return to her village that had forced her out when she was sick. So Sister Li went with her. As the young woman walked through the small village, people came out of their homes and stared. 'Could this be the same woman?' they wondered. 'How is she suddenly healed?'

"Sister Li and the woman told the villagers about the healing power of Jesus. And twenty-two people in that small village in Tibet gave their lives to Him."

"Wow," Shan sighed.

"Oh yeah." Yang clapped his hooves even louder.

Fay bowed.

FuFu held up the pot. "More tea?"

"Remember, Master Shan," a raspy voice began. Shan jumped back from the red panda that seemed to appear from nowhere.

"He does that," Yang said, not even looking up.

"Be strong and courageous, Master Shan! 'Do not tremble or be dismayed, for the Lord your God is with you wherever you go.'"

"Ah, yes, Old Red." FuFu nodded. "Joshua 1:9."

Shan nodded too. He understood . . . well, at least, he was beginning to. He took another sip of tea, trying to soak in all that he had seen and heard, there in the bamboo forest.

That afternoon, Shan welcomed his parents home with hugs. He told them about the bamboo forest and the cave, but left out the part about the tea-serving panda, the talking takin, the traveling bird, and the wise Old Red. He supposed he would keep that to himself for now.

Before bed that night, Shan thanked God for his parents and new friends. He thanked Him for His constant protection. And he asked God to help him be obedient, no matter what.

Then Shan lay there alone, watching the twinkling night sky, feeling very small—and yet, very brave.